CW00540677

Text: *Dennis Kelsall*
Series editor: *Tony Bowerman*
Photographs: *Dennis Kelsall, Karen Frenkel/*
www.karenfrenkel.info, Shutterstock,
Dreamstime, Bigstock

Design: *Carl Rogers*

© *Northern Eye Books Limited 2015*

Northern Eye Books

ISBN 978-1-908632-07-4

*A CIP catalogue record for this book is available
from the British Library.*

www.northerneyebooks.co.uk

Cover: *Dove Dale's famous
stepping-stones (Walk 10)*

First published in 2015 by

Northern Eye Books Limited
*High Street, Tattenhall,
Cheshire CH3 9PX*

Email: tony@northerneyebooks.com

For sales enquiries, please call 01928 723 744

 Twitter: @Northerneyeboo
@Top10walks

Contents

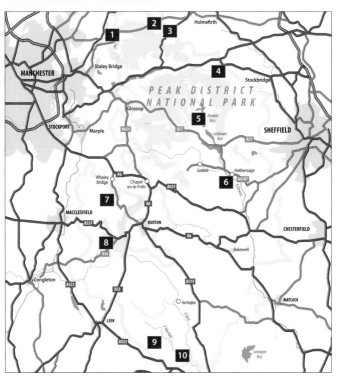

Britain's First National Park

CREATED IN 1951, THE PEAK DISTRICT NATIONAL PARK extends over six counties and is the second most visited of Britain's National Parks. Its highest point lies upon the seemingly remote Kinder plateau, where a mass trespass in 1932 marked the turning point in a long and sometimes bitter campaign that led to the creation of Britain's National Parks and the open access we enjoy today.

The high, peaty moorlands of the northern Dark Peak are founded on gritstone, their stark grandeur accentuated by weatherworn tors and edges. The moors extend out of the Pennines in two horns that enclose the limestone plateau of the White Peak, an upland pasture deeply cleft by narrow gorges and dales. The transition between the two is startlingly abrupt and each has a distinctive character and beauty all its own; the wild openness of the north contrasting with a more intimate landscape dotted with small villages and criss-crossed by old lanes.

Ladybower Reservoir

Rivers and reservoirs

Several major rivers originate in the Peak, fed by countless
springs, brooks and streams that have cut deep cloughs
and gorges through the grit and limestone. Many
powered the early industrialisation of the area while
the valleys often served as conduits for trans-Pennine
trade. Other dales, too steep or narrow for settlement or
farming, or whose streams found subterranean courses,
were ignored and today provide valuable wildlife habitats.
And although the region has no significant natural lakes,
reservoirs abound and are now largely naturalised within
the landscape.

"Within ten or twelve miles of Manchester
… is this tract of mountain land abounding
with springs of the purest quality."

J F Bateman's report for the Manchester Corporation, 1846

TOP 10 **Walks:** Waterside Walks

MOST WALKS WITHIN THE PEAK DISTRICT will encounter water at some point. But there are places where a spring, stream or river and the clough or dale through which it flows is a particular highlight, while many of the reservoirs occupy stunningly dramatic or scenic locations. Those featured here explore the diversity of the Peak's waterside settings, ranging from the evocative remoteness of high moorland to the intimacy of secluded dales.

Dove Stone Reservoir — page 8

Digley Reservoir — page 12

The Ramsden Valley — page 18

Langsett Reservoir — page 24

The view across Dove Stone Reservoir to Alderman's Hill

Dove Stone Reservoir

An easy but spectacular lakeside walk below the edges of Saddleworth Moor

Distance/time: 6.5km/ 4 miles. Allow 2 hours

Start: Dove Stone pay and display car park

Grid ref: SE 013 034

Ordnance Survey Map: Explorer OL1 *The Peak District: Dark Peak area: Kinder Scout, Bleaklow, Black Hill & Ladybower Reservoir*

After the walk: The Clarence, Chew Valley Road, Greenfield OL3 7DD | 01457 872319

What to expect:
Easy-access paths and tracks beside the Dove Stone Reservoir, becoming grass beside Yeoman Hey

Walk outline
Slicing through the heart of Saddleworth Moor, the deep narrow rift of the Greenfield valley is an impressive backdrop to the chain of reservoirs stepped within its base. Beginning at the foot of Dove Stone, the lowest of the reservoirs, the route gently climbs along the valley, overlooked by the striking outcrops of the Dove Stone Edge. Rounding the Yeoman Hey Reservoir beneath the Greenfield Dam, the walk returns along the western bank.

Dove Stone outlet tower

The Greenfield valley
Opened in 1967, Dove Stone is the lowest, largest and last to be built of the major reservoirs within the Greenfield valley. Yeoman Hey and Greenfield lie farther along the narrowing fold while a fourth, Chew Reservoir sits on the moor above. That was completed in 1912 and, with Cow Green in County Durham (opened 1971), is the highest in England. Between them, the Greenfield reservoirs supply water to Oldham, with Dove Stone also used for sailing. The impressive craggy edge above is studded with a succession of jagged outcrops that include Great Dove Stone Rocks and the Trinnacle, a detached, fragmented rock pillar above the Greenfield Reservoir.

Mountain hare

The Walk

1. Follow the broad track from the upper end of the car park around the southern shore of the reservoir, passing the **Dove Stone Sailing Club's pavilion** and boat store.

2. At a junction just beyond the bridge over **Chew Brook**, branch left to cross a second bridge. The curving shoreline opens a view across the water to the striking profile of Alderman's Hill. Keep ahead through a gate by a lone silver birch, the path running below the towering cliffs of **Great Dove Stone Rocks**. Carry on beside a conifer plantation to a picnic area at the foot of **Ashway Gap**.

3. Cross a bridge over the stream. *Much of its water actually comes from Birchen Clough farther up the valley, bypassing the Greenfield and Yeoman Hey reservoirs within a tunnel bored beneath the hill.*

Walk on towards the **Yeoman Hey Dam**. Just before a bridge across the overspill, bear right onto a grass path, which undulates across the hillside below **Ashway Rocks**. Continue beyond the head of the lake, eventually dropping to a bridge over the waterspill at the foot of the **Greenfield Dam**.

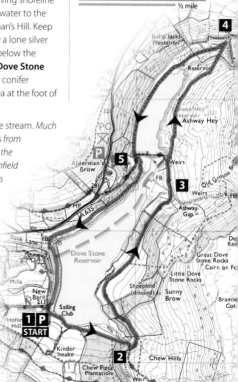

Reflective mood: *High, wispy summer clouds mirrored in Dove Stone Reservoir*

4. On the northern bank, go left and then keep left at a fork to head back down the valley.

The way later joins the main service track to reach the **Yeoman Hey Dam**.

5. Remain on this side of the valley, but then leave the main drive after just a few metres through a kissing-gate on the left. A gravel path falls to follow the western shore of the **Dove Stone Reservoir**. After passing the reservoir outflow tower, drop left to a bridge and follow the onward path across the top of the dam back to complete the walk. ♦

Ashway Gap House

A long-gone Gothic mansion once stood at the foot of Ashway Gap: a shooting lodge built in 1850 for the wealthy Oldham businessman John Platt. Following the death of his brother James — who was MP for the town — in a shooting accident, he shunned the place. The lodge was eventually taken over by the Ashton, Stalybridge and Dukinfield Waterworks Joint Committee, whose markers stand beside the path.

Autumn tints fringe the calm surface of Digley Reservoir

Digley Reservoir

A grand lake and moorland walk in the upper reaches of the Holme valley

Distance/time: 9.5km/ 6 miles. Allow 3 hours

Start: Digley Reservoir car park

Grid ref: SE 109 067

Ordnance Survey Map: Explorer OL1 *The Peak District: Dark Peak area: Kinder Scout, Bleaklow, Black Hill & Ladybower Reservoir*

After the walk: The Fleece Inn, Woodhead Road, Holme Holmfirth HD9 2QG | 01484 683449 | shirley@fleeceinnholme.co.uk

What to expect:
Clear paths and moorland tracks

Walk outline

Setting the scene, the route encircles the Digley Reservoir before climbing through a pretty clough above the southern bank. Old tracks take the way onto the open moor beneath the steep slopes of Black Hill, crossing Hey Clough and eventually dropping into the confines of Marsden Clough. After a short pull out of the valley, it is then easy walking across the hillside back to Digley.

Digley Reservoir

The Bilberry Reservoir was constructed in 1840 to secure water for the many mills in the valley. Tragically, it burst during a storm in 1852, the deluge killing 81 people in Holmfirth. Although rebuilt, it became insufficient to meet the demands of growing industrialisation and urbanisation and the Digley Reservoir was commissioned in 1938. However, unforeseen difficulties and delays meant that it was not completed until 1953. The rising waters drowned two mills, one of which was already derelict. Occasionally when the water level is low, ruined walls can be seen. Bilberry now serves to collect silt that would otherwise be washed into the main reservoir.

Bench with a view

Nesting lapwing

The Walk

1. Follow the lane across the **dam** to a junction. Go left, and then leave on the bend through a gate on the left. A path leads through a pleasant picnic area, climbing steps to meet a track above **Digley Quarry car park**.

2. Follow it left past disused quarry workings and a conifer plantation. Descending towards the reservoir, watch for a right fork, the path temporarily leaving the old lane, which was flooded when the reservoir was filled. Soon descending steps, the path skirts a small inlet and then rises to rejoin the original track. Wind on to a fork above the **Bilberry Dam**.

3. Drop left into the valley, cross on the old dam and follow the ongoing path left, up through **Lumbank Wood**. Pass through a gate and continue to a second gate.

4. Instead of going through, turn right beside the wall to a stile and carry on above a delightful clough in which the stream cascades over a small **waterfall**. Arriving at the sharp bend of a track, take the left branch, which winds easily up the hillside for 400 metres/¼ mile.

5. Reaching a junction, go right. Levelling beyond a bench, well-placed to enjoy the view down the Holme valley, the track runs arrow straight towards the rearing bulk of **Black Hill**.

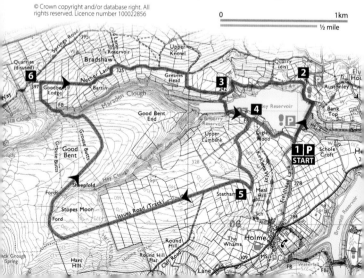

Water power: *Victorian Bilberry Dam once supplied water to the mills in the valley below*

Now forever linked with Foggy, Compo and Clegg, the Holme Valley was widely used for location shots throughout the BBC television series 'Last of the Summer Wine'. Although the camera crews have long gone, Holmfirth still acts as a magnet for the show's fans from around the world and you can still have a cuppa in Sid's Café or even stay in Nora Batty's house. But the cloughs at the head of the valley are largely deserted, old field walls and isolated cottages relics of a past way of life. In the cool, wet climate, farming only ever provided a meagre existence and the mainstay of income was derived from handloom weaving. Though a cottage industry, it was highly organised. Yarn was regularly brought in and cloth taken away to market by merchants along the network of ancient tracks and many of the cottages have long rows of mullioned windows to let light into the loom rooms. An architectural curiosity of the area are the four storey 'double decker' cottages built into the hillside, the ground accessed from the front while the upper floor was reached by steep stairs at the back.

Flooded valley: *Heather, bilberry, birch and conifer plantations fringe Digley Reservoir*

Ignoring a junction, keep ahead through a gate, later passing through a second gate onto the open moor. After some 400 metres/¼ mile bear right at a waymarked fork to curve above **Hey Clough**.

Shortly fording the stream, the track continues above the northern bank of the deepening fold before turning across the shoulder of **Good Bent**. Descend to **Blackpool Bridge** at the head of **Marsden Clough** and zigzag with the main track up the far bank to a stile beside a gate. Walk away by the left

wall to leave at the field's far side onto another track, **Nether Lane**.

Sometimes going by the name of 'peewit' in imitation of its shrill call, the lapwing was once a common sight on farmland, nesting in hollows on open, newly planted ground, rough grazing or marsh. The shift to autumn planting and 'improved' pasture led to a general decline during the latter part of the 20th century, but there are places where it is making a comeback. Coloured black with a white breast and sporting a crest, it is easily recognised, and though its stubby wings might seem ungainly, its tumbling, aerobatic display flight is a delight to watch.

6. Heading right, there is a fine view along the valley. In 1.2 kilometres/¾ mile, at a junction, turn right. Swinging through a sharp left bend, the track carries on above **Bilberry Reservoir**. At the junction passed on the way out (**3**), double back down to re-cross the dam. Climb through **Lumbank Wood**, but this time, when you reach the gate by the stream (**4**), go through and follow the path overlooking **Digley Reservoir** back to the car park to complete the walk. ◆

A long lost landscape

Although isolated today, the hills around Holme valley were once busy. Crumbling walls mark old field boundaries while a network of tracks and lanes connect the now abandoned farmsteads and quarries. At Black Pool, the substantial buttresses of the original bridge that took the lane across Marsden Clough can still be seen, built to carry heavy carts laden with stone from the quarries above.

Looking down over Riding Wood Reservoir

The **Ramsden Valley**

Lakeside, forest and moor from the tiny Pennine village of Holme

Distance/time: 7km/ 4½ miles. Allow 2½ hours

Start: Ramsden Reservoir car park

Grid ref: SE 115 056

Ordnance Survey Map: Explorer OL1 *The Peak District: Dark Peak area: Kinder Scout, Bleaklow, Black Hill & Ladybower Reservoir*

After the walk: The Fleece Inn, Woodhead Road, Holme Holmfirth HD9 2QG | 01484 683449 | shirley@fleeceinnholme.co.uk

What to expect:
Clear paths and moorland paths with a couple of steeper ascents

Walk outline

A roundabout start takes in the woodland above Ramsden Reservoir before crossing the dam of Riding Wood and skirting the base of the high grass bank holding back Yateholme. Continuing through forest, the way winds above Netherley Clough before dropping into the neighbouring valley at Gill Hey Bridge. After visiting Holme, where there is a pub, the route re-crosses Rake Dike and encircles the Ramsden Reservoir to return to the start.

The Ramsden valley

Gathering the innumerable springs and streams flowing off Holme Moss, Ramsden Clough and its several tributaries combine in a great bowl, scooped from the high plateau above. Tucked within are four separate reservoirs, the highest three being built during the latter part of the 19th century to ensure water for the mills and homes of the expanding towns on the eastern flank of the Pennines. Brownhill, the lowest of the group, was opened in 1932. Surrounded by forest and fed by deep, heathery cloughs, they provide a picturesque setting for the walk.

Steps to Gill Hey Bridge

Small heath butterfly

The Walk

1. Leaving the car park, go right and right again along a rising track beside the picnic area. At a fork, keep right to stay with the edge of the forest. Reaching a bend, swing right in front of a stile and continue up to meet the bend of a track. Follow it downhill into the trees to a junction in front of a cottage.

2. Go left, keeping with the track as it then turns across the dam of the **Riding** **Wood Reservoir**. Continue through more trees, shortly curving beneath the high grass bank of the **Yateholme Dam**. Heading into the trees beyond, the track crosses **Gusset Dike** and then twists sharply right to cross **Netherley Dike**. Carry on for a further 800 metres/½ mile, gently descending through the trees to rough moorland grazing.

3. Rounding a bend, look for a stile on the right. Head directly away across a sometimes-marshy patch of ground. After 100 metres, watch for a stile breaking the fence on the right. However, instead of crossing, turn away to the left. Follow the curve of a crumbling wall towards Holme, seen on the hillside in the middle distance. Over a stile, a stepped path

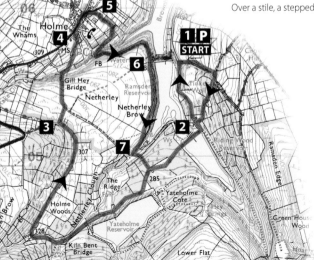

0 _____ 1km

_____ ½ mile

Woodland waterfall: *Rake Dike Bridge is deep in the woods*

descends a steep birch and heather-clad bank to **Gill Hey Bridge**. After climbing from the clough, the path continues across sloping pastures towards a white cottage. Leave through its garden and walk out onto **Holme**'s main street.

4. Head right past the **Fleece Inn** and **Pantry** through the heart of the village. Keep right at a fork in front of the old school house, but then after 100 metres, turn off along a narrow track beside the entrance to **Underhill**.

The village's first school was built in 1694, funded under a charity bequeathed by Joshua Earnshaw so that the village children could receive free tuition in English and Latin. However, by the 19th century, the building had become dilapidated and was rebuilt in 1838. The school subsequently moved to other premises but the building continued in use as the Sunday School. Date stones record its original foundation and subsequent rebuilding and adaptation, while an inscribed corbel on the corner points the way to neighbouring villages.

Valley view: *Ramsden Reservoir sits in a deep wooded valley surrounded by open hills*

5. Through a gate at the end, walk on at the field edge. *As you do, glance back to see one of Britain's first modern 'earth houses', which was designed by the architect Arthur Quarmby in 1978.* Slip through a gate to continue on the opposite side of the wall down to a stile. A trod strikes across a sloping pasture to a second stile, from which a path runs above a steep, wooded fold enclosing **Rake Dike**. Drop to a bridge above a small waterfall, cross the stream and climb away to the left. Emerging onto the edge of heath, the path rounds

the snout of **Netherley Hill** before descending into more trees.

6. Watch for a fork (just before reaching railings) and branch right. Leaving the wood, pass through a gap in a stone wall above the dam holding back the **Ramsden Reservoir**.

Carry on across the open hillside, eventually crossing another wall beyond the head of the lake. Branch left at a fork, the path falling into **Netherley Clough**, where a bridge takes the way across the stream.

7. Climb the opposite slope, passing through a gate gap into the plantation

above. Continue up through the trees to a wall stile at the top. Meeting a track, turn left and follow it back across the **Riding Wood Dam**.

Swing left to pass the cottage **(2)**, but this time keep with the track ahead to return to the car park and complete the walk ♦

The Ramsden family and the Holme valley

The Ramsdens had been lords of the extensive manor since the 16th century and supported Huddersfield's expansion as an industrial town. They built a cloth hall and canal and later encouraged the railway, but it was Sir John Ramsden who recognised the importance of the Holme valley in building the first waterworks in 1743. The Ramsdens eventually sold their estate to Huddersfield Corporation in 1920.

The castellated outflow tower at Langsett Reservoir

Langsett Reservoir

Waterside and woodland at the edge of the Peak District's eastern moor

Distance/time: 6km/ 3¾ miles. Allow 2 hours

Start: Langsett Barn car park

Grid ref: SE 211 004

Ordnance Survey Map: Explorer OL1 *The Peak District: Dark Peak area: Kinder Scout, Bleaklow, Black Hill & Ladybower Reservoir*

After the walk: Waggon and Horses, Main Road, Langsett S36 4GY
01226 763147 | info@langsettinn.com

What to expect:
Clear tracks and woodland paths, a gentle climb

Walk outline

From the settlement of Langsett, overlooking the valley of the Little Don River, the walk begins across the dam that created a lake within the deep and narrow valley. Taking to the woods below Upper Midhope, the route follows the shore to Thickwoods Brook, then climbs onto the open moor past the ruin of North America Farm. After descending to cross the Little Don, the walk returns through the conifer plantation of Langsett Bank above the northern shoreline.

Langsett

Once held by Kirkstead Abbey in Lincolnshire, Langsett grew as a farming community beside old packhorse routes. The great winter store barn beside the car park was built in 1621, its large double doors enabling loaded wagons to pass inside. The character of the valley changed at the end of the 19th century with the construction of a reservoir to supply the growing conurbations of Sheffield and Barnsley. A temporary village housed workers brought in for the job and a railway was built to transport materials. The village was 'invaded' again during the Second World War, when the surrounding moors were used for tank training.

Langsett Bank

Long-eared owl

The Walk

1. Leaving the car park past **Langsett Barn**, wind through the cluster of cottages and converted barns to meet the main road beside the **Waggon and Horses**. Turn right and then right again along a lane towards Strines and the Derwent Valley. It swings to cross the top of the **dam** beneath a crenellated house, built for the reservoir manager. On the far side of the valley, bend left past a small disused quarry, concealed within the edge of a wood.

2. After 200 metres, leave beside a bridleway track on the right, passing through a narrow gap between wall and fence into the corner of a wood. Take the right hand one of the two paths, winding back above the quarry and then following a fence left above the **lake**. Carry on for just over 800 metres/ ½ mile, eventually emerging beyond the trees onto a gravel track.

3. To the right after passing through a gate, the track shortly bends across a bridge over **Thickwoods Brook**. Climb away past **Mauk Royd**, in time leaving the plantation fringe and rising to a gate at the edge of the open moor.

4. Through the gate, continue past the ruin of **North America Farm** across **Hingcliff Common**. Later meeting a junction of paths, turn right. Head gently downhill towards the corner of the woodland fringe bordering the lake. The path steepens beside the trees, winding down to a bridge across the **Little Don**

0	1km
	½ mile

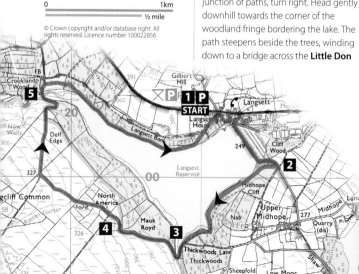

Room with a view?: *All that remains of North America Farm today is a pile of stones*

River. The clough is a pretty spot and ideal for a riverside picnic.

5. Over the bridge, climb away on a track. After 50 metres, just before the gradient eases, take a footpath signed off on the right. Beyond a fringe of birch the way delves into a mature plantation dominated by towering pine. Remaining in sight of the shore, the path runs across the steep slope of **Langsett Bank**. Walk for 1.2 kilometres/¾ mile to a fork. Take the left branch, gaining height through the trees to join a higher path. Follow it right back to the car park to complete the walk. ♦

All for clean water

Until the introduction of water treatment plants, reservoir catchments were largely cleared of people and livestock to ensure water purity, leaving farmsteads such as 'North America' empty and abandoned. Fringing conifers helped filter the water while also providing a return as a cash crop. Today, many forests are being replanted with native species such as oak and birch, which support a greater variety of wildlife.

Derwent Reservoir on a still, warm summer's day

Derwent Reservoir

An easy ramble along the less-visited eastern banks of the Upper Derwent's picturesque reservoirs

What to expect:
Good tracks throughout, best done at weekend when the shuttle bus is running

Distance: 9km/ 5½miles. Allow 2½ hours

Start: Fairholmes Visitor Centre pay and display car park, Derwent

Grid ref: SK 172 893/SK 167 938

Ordnance Survey Map: Explorer OL1 *The Peak District: Dark Peak area: Kinder Scout, Bleaklow, Black Hill & Ladybower Reservoir*

After the walk: Light refreshments at the Visitor Centre, OR Ladybower Inn, Bamford S33 0AX | 01433 651 241 info@ladybower-inn.co.uk

Walk outline

Weekend and bank holiday buses operate between the Fairholmes Visitor Centre and King's Tree near the northern tip of the Howden Reservoir. The walk then follows the track north to Slippery Stones, crossing the river to meander above the eastern bank of Howden and Derwent back to Fairholmes. Mid-week, cars have access to King's Tree, where roadside parking enables a 'there and back' walk. Alternatively, the route is ideal for family cycling.

National Trust sign

The Upper Derwent Valley

Until the construction of the reservoirs at the beginning of the 20th century, the Upper Derwent Valley was an isolated place. The lane did not go much farther up the valley than Derwent Chapel, its only village and which grew up around a monastic grange founded by Welbeck Abbey near Worksop in Nottinghamshire around the 12th century. Winding some 16 kilometres/10 miles into the deserted moorland of Hope Forest, the Derwent is the longest High Peak's valley without a through road. Even today, it is a quiet and seemingly remote place and its higher reaches above the tip of Howden are relatively little visited.

Common sandpiper

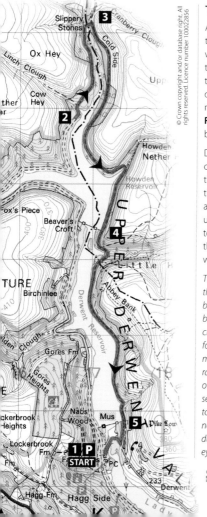

The Walk

At weekends and on bank holidays, the narrow lane up the valley on the western side of the reservoirs beyond the **Fairholmes Visitor Centre** is closed to traffic. Instead, a shuttle bus service operates to **King's Tree (2)**, which lies near the northern tip of the **Howden Reservoir** and where the walking begins.

During the week, unless able to leave a car at either end, you can park beside the lane at King's Tree **(2)** and follow the route as far as inclination dictates and then return. The remoteness of the upper section of the valley is something to be savoured and the perspective of the views completely changes on the way back.

The combination of habitats makes the Derwent Valley a great place for birdwatching. The trees and feeders draw blue and coal tits, nuthatch, siskin and crossbill, and in the upper valley, look out for dippers and meadow pipit. The open moors attract curlew, ring ouzel and ravens with hunters such as short-eared owls, hen harriers and perhaps goshawks searching for a meal. There's a chance too of seeing a peregrine; they nest on the nearby cliffs of Alport Castles. Amongst the ducks on the water, watch out for golden eye or even red-breasted merganser.

0   1km

1 mile

Quiet shore: *Derwent Reservoir in summer*

1. At weekends, park at **Fairholmes** and take the bus to **King's Tree** (SK 167 938).

2. Walk through the gate at the end of the turning circle and follow the ongoing track, signed as a bridleway to 'Slippery Stones'. After crossing the stream flowing out of **Linch Clough**, the trail leaves the lakeshore to rise over a wooded shoulder. Beyond, hidden behind the trees below, the tip of the lake progressively narrows to become the inflowing stream of the **River**

Derwent. Later, at a fork, keep left, the track then soon falling through a bridle gate to a **packhorse bridge** over the river at **Slippery Stones**.

The graceful 17th-century packhorse bridge originally spanned the river below Derwent Chapel, but was dismantled before the valley was flooded and rebuilt here in 1959.

3. Follow the ongoing track away to the left to a junction. Turn right, the way signed as the ' Derwent Valley Cycle Trail'. A broad track, it climbs gently across the steep slope of **Cold Side**. There is a fine

Green fringe: *Water-filtering conifers edge the mighty Howden Reservoir*

view along the valley, while below, the winding **River Derwent** becomes lost in the **Howden Reservoir**. Farther on, the lake disappears behind trees bordering the route. Eventually the track curves around to cross the foot of **Howden Clough**. Continue towards the **Howden Dam**, which can be glimpsed through the trees.

Howden was the first of the Derwent Valley dams to be built. It was begun in 1901 with the Derwent being started the following year. They were completed in 1912 and 1914 respectively but quickly proved inadequate to meet the demands. Tunnels were subsequently dug to bring across additional water from the neighbouring Ashop and Alport valleys. In 1935, work began on the Ladybower Reservoir. When it was completed in 1945, the valley contained the largest area of man-made lake in Europe at the time.

4. Passing the high dam, the track descends to wind across the foot of **Abbey Brook**. The trail resumes its southerly heading, the bounding trees soon giving way to reveal the **Derwent Reservoir**. Eventually, after crossing streams descending out of **Walker's**

Clough and **Hollins Clough**, the track passes beside the **Derwent Dam**.

5. As the track then begins to descend, take a path on the right, which drops from the trees to meet a narrow lane.

Follow it right beneath the high wall of the dam and across the overflow stream. Just beyond, a path on the left leads to the **Fairholmes Visitor Centre** and car park, completing the walk. ♦

The 'Dambusters'

Derwent Reservoir was one of the training grounds for 617 Squadron: the 'Dambusters', tasked in 1943 with destroying the Möhne and Eder dams in Germany's industrial heartland. Flying at 240mph, 18 metres above the water demanded great skill. Only seven of the nineteen Lancaster bombers reached the target; eight were shot down or crashed. Contrary to British propaganda, the attack achieved only limited success.

The River Derwent in autumn

The **River Derwent**

The pastoral flanks of Offerton Moor give splendid views across the Derwent Valley

What to expect:
Farm tracks, field paths and fine riverside walks, but with a short pull to Offerton Hall

Distance/time: 9km/ 5½ miles. Allow 3 hours

Start: Shatton, considerate roadside parking

Grid ref: SK 203 825

Ordnance Survey Map: Explorer OL1 *The Peak District: Dark Peak area: Kinder Scout, Bleaklow, Black Hill & Ladybower Reservoir*

After the walk: The Plough Inn, Leadmill Bridge, Hathersage S32 1BA | 01433 650319 | sales@theploughinn-hathersage.co.uk

Walk outline

Beginning at Shatton beside the River Noe by its confluence with the River Derwent, the walk climbs across the fields to pick up a track to Offerton Hall. Shortly taking to the fields again, the route drops through a wooded valley above Dunge Brook and on down to the banks of the Derwent near Leadmill Bridge. After visiting the pub there, the return follows the river upstream all the way back to Shatton.

The Derwent Valley

Away from the narrow confines of the Upper Derwent Valley the river meanders through a flat-bottomed valley bordered by trees and grazing meadows. And, although both the main road and railway find space as well, the walk reveals a bucolic facet of the Peak District's landscape.

In Goose Nest Wood

There is a sense of history too, for along the way the old hall at Offerton, ancient tracks and stepping-stones across the river are reminders of a way of life that has all but gone. Another relic of the past lies only a short distance from the route: the shaft of an ancient way cross dating from at least the 17th century and known as Robin Hood's Stoop.

Dipper

Question of balance: *Ancient stepping stones arc across the River Derwent*

The Walk

1. Walk back towards the main road, leaving the lane immediately before the bridge across the **River Noe** through a pinch stile on the right. A path signed to 'Leadmill' leads across a pretty side stream. Where the path then forks, branch right and rise across rough pasture to a stile. Walk upfield by the right-hand boundary, emerging over a stile at the top onto a narrow lane.

2. Following it left, there is a view across to the long line of impressive escarpments that step back in tiers above the northern flank of the valley. Where the lane shortly swings right into **Garner House Farm**, keep ahead through a gate on a field track signed to 'Offerton'. The way continues at the edge of successive pastures, gently rising to a crest where Offerton Hall comes into view. The track dips sharply to cross a diminutive stream flowing from **Old Clough**. At a junction keep right, climbing steeply to **Offerton**

Hall. Remain with the main track as it winds between the several buildings, levelling beyond to run high along the valley side.

3. After 400 metres/¼ mile, watch for a path leaving over a stile on the left.

To see **Robin Hood's Stoop**, *walk along the lane for a further 200 metres; it stands in the field to the right.*

Climbing the stile, the path descends across hawthorn scrub into a small wood, there crossing a stream. Emerging from the trees, cross another meadow to come out onto a track at **Callow Farm**. Go left and then turn right through the middle one of three gates. A trod drops through a gap in an intervening wall

to a gate at the edge of a walled wood. The ongoing path angles down across the steep, wooded valley-side of **Dunge Brook**. Beyond the trees, carry on across a sloping meadow to emerge through a gate at the bottom onto a track.

4. Go right, across **Dunge Brook** and climb away to meet the end of a lane at the entrance to **Mount Pleasant Farm**. Pass through a gate on the left and take a slanting course down the field towards the corner of a wood. Keep ahead with the boundary wall on your left. Walk on in a second field until you reach a wall stile. Over that, the path drops steeply down a wooded bank and then heads across a meadow to join a path beside the **River Derwent** near a derelict shed.

How green was my valley: *The lovely open farmland of the lower Derwent Valley*

For refreshment, continue downstream to **Leadmill Bridge**, there clambering out over a stile onto the road. *The lead mill which gave the bridge its name was originally built to grind corn and finally ended up as a stone mason's yard, the wheel then being used to power a saw and dressing hammer.* The **Plough Inn** lies a short distance up to the right.

5. Retrace your steps from the pub to the riverbank and head back upstream, passing a **weir** that impounded water to power the lead mill. The path shortly passes into **Goose Nest Wood**, where the banks are thickly carpeted with wild garlic and bluebells in late spring.

Emerging from the trees, the path runs beside more pastures and, rounding a bend, brings **Nether Hall** on the opposite bank into view.

Some 1.2km/¾ mile farther on, below **Offerton Hall**, there are **stepping-stones** across the river, but the way remains on this bank. Just beyond, the path rises up steps and along the top of a high cliff above the river, angling down through a wood at the far side to cross the foot of **Old Clough**.

6. The way continues beside the river at the edge of grazing, eventually passing into the fringe of more woodland where the **confluence of the Derwent with the Noe** is largely obscured by trees.

Meeting your outward path, carry on over the side stream to return to the lane at the edge of **Shatton** and complete the walk. ◆

The Eyres of Hathersage

Offerton Hall was one of seven Elizabethan halls built by Robert Eyre of Highlow for his sons. An important Norman family, they had been hereditary wardens over the Royal Forest of the Peak. The family memorials in Hathersage's church gave Charlotte Brontë a name for her latest heroine when she was a guest at the vicarage in 1845. In her novel, the town became Morton and nearby North Lees Hall, Thornfield Hall.

Fernilee's distinctive pumphouse

Fernilee Reservoir

Forest and waterside come together in this splendid walk along a quiet section of the Goyt Valley

What to expect:
Clear woodland tracks and paths, but which may be muddy in places after heavy rain

Distance/time: 6.5km/ 4 miles. Allow 2 hours

Start: Goyt Forest car park, above Errwood Dam

Grid ref: SK 013 756

Ordnance Survey Map: Explorer OL24 *Peak District: White Peak area: Buxton, Bakewell, Matlock & Dove Dale*

After the walk: Cat and Fiddle, summit of the A537 Buxton Road SK11 0AR | 01298 78366 | info@catandfiddleinn.com

Walk outline

After climbing the lane from the car park, the walk undulates easily across the steep, forested slope of Hoo Moor. Emerging from the trees, old farm tracks lead to Normanwood, where the way descends towards the deep-sided valley of Mill Clough. Swinging south, the return traces the flank of the Goyt Valley to the Fernilee Dam. Continuing into the trees, the way soon descends to the shore, following it up the valley back to the Errwood Dam.

The Goyt Valley reservoirs

Rising on the moors of Axe Edge, the River Goyt anciently served as a boundary between the Norman royal hunting forests of Macclesfield and of the Peak, which lay to the east. By the 19th century, the valley contained a busy farming and industrial community, connected by a railway that linked the Peak Forest and Cromford canals. But the growth of Stockport demanded ever-increasing supplies of water, and the Town Corporation acquired the valley for the construction of two reservoirs. Fernilee was completed in 1938 with Errwood following in 1967, changing the character of the valley forever.

Stream crossing

Pipistrelle bat

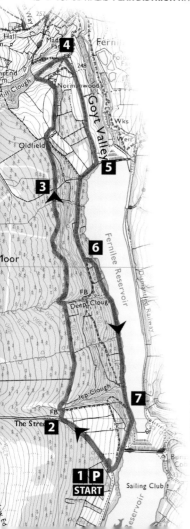

The Walk

1. Leaving the top end of the car park, head uphill beside the lane. As the path ends, cross to a gated track opposite.

From its source high on the hill behind the Cat and Fiddle, the River Goyt quickly drops from the open moor to cleave a deep, narrow valley through ancient shale, grit and sandstone. The hard stone was used as mill- and grindstones as well as for roof and paving flags and before the railways, was carted out on the backs of packhorses. William Pickford started his haulage business here in the early 17th century; carrying stone to all parts of the country and returning with loads inbound for Manchester.

2. Part of the **Mid-Shires Way** and signed to 'Hoo Moor', the trail winds into the forest, where spruce, pine, larch and birch overshadow an under-carpet of bilberry. Eventually the trees thin to reveal the dam of the **Fernilee Reservoir** far below.

The forests of conifers overlooking the reservoir were planted from 1965 and, now reaching maturity, will be selectively felled. Breaking the uniform planting in the many cloughs that cut the hillside are stands of older woodland where native oak and

0   1km

                   ½ mile

Moving light: *Sunlight and shadow move across the Goyt Valley and Fernilee Reservoir*

birch can be found. These are the places to look for birds such as nuthatch, tree creepers, woodpeckers and jays. Down by the water's edge, you might see common sandpipers while the lake itself attracts Canada geese and a variety of ducks. In the quietness of dusk, keep your eyes open for bats, foxes and badgers and if you are really lucky, you just might spot a red deer.

3. Leave the far end of the forest through a gate and walk on to join a track rising from the dam. Follow it through another gate and past **Oldfield Farm**, continuing to the yard of **Normanwood**. Through the gate ahead, the track descends to a sharp bend. Turn with it through a second gate and carry on, losing height across the slope of **Mill Clough** beside a plantation of larch.

4. Emerging onto a crossing track, go right, passing through a gate beside **Knipe Farm**. Remain with the main track along the steep side of the **Goyt Valley**. Walk on for nearly 800 metres/½ mile to a junction beside the **Fernilee Dam**.

Rolling hills: *Panoramic views suddenly open out across the Goyt Valley*

5. Go right on a narrow track towards 'Old Field Farm'. However, where it then curves right, fork off through a gate into the forest on a path signed to 'Errwood'.

6. After 400 metres/¼ mile, immediately after fording a small stream, branch left on a descending path marked as the 'Waterside Walk'. Winding down steeply, it soon reaches the **Fernilee Reservoir**. Continue above the shoreline, occasionally twisting across the foot of narrow cloughs bringing small streams from the hillside above. *Attached to*

some of the tree trunks are boxes, placed to encourage breeding bats.

7. Shortly after crossing the foot of **Jep Clough** and approaching the steep grass bank of the **Errwood Dam**, watch for a path forking right and marked to 'Errwood'.

Nearby Errwood Hall was built around 1840 by Samuel Grimshawe, whose family were manufacturers and merchants in Manchester. Built in the Italianate style, the hall hosted many grand social events. They were also great benefactors showing great consideration to the people who lived and worked on their estate. After the death of

the last of the family, Mary Grimshawe, in 1930, the estate was sold to Stockport Council. For a time the house was run as a youth hostel, but as the reservoir was nearing completion it was demolished to avoid the risk of pollution.

Climb out of the trees and continue across pasture, to meet the lane above the dam at a junction by the car park's lower entrance to complete the walk. ♦

The Goyt Valley

Until the 1930s, paint and gunpowder factories, quarries and coal mines all lay within the valley, with farms and a country house dotted across the hillsides. All were demolished to make way for the reservoirs. Half a century on, the landscape has naturalised and the maturing conifer plantations are being replanted with native broadleaf trees that support a rich diversity of wildflowers, birds and mammals.

Three Shire Heads and Panniers Pool

Three Shire Heads

Stunning walk to a pretty waterfall and packhorse bridge, at the meeting point of three county boundaries

Distance/time: 9.5km/ 6 miles. Allow 3 hours

Start: Wildboarclough, small roadside car park beside the bridge

Grid ref: SJ 982 687

Ordnance Survey Map: Explorer OL24 *Peak District: White Peak area: Buxton, Bakewell, Matlock & Dove Dale*

After the walk: Crag Inn (close to the start), Wildboarclough SK11 0BD | 01260 227239

What to expect:
Clear but occasionally rugged moorland paths. A sustained climb from the start

Walk outline

After rising over Banktop to avoid the lane, the route crosses Clough Brook and climbs onto the moor along the pretty valley of Cumberland Brook. Dropping through Danebower Hollow, the way joins the River Dane to Three Shire Heads. Contouring out of the valley past Cut-thorn, the path crosses the moorland shoulder into the Wildboarclough valley, descending beside Crag Hall estate back to the river.

Clough Brook and the River Dane

Although thickly wooded lower down, the upper reaches of the River Dane, as it flows off Axe Moor, cut a deep valley through a dramatically bare landscape. In sharp contrast, the early part of the walk is above Clough Brook, although its gentle pastoral and wooded setting can be deceiving. The valley's name perhaps does not refer to wild boars but instead to the savage bore of water that can rage down the valley after heavy rain. In 1816, four bridges and 3 kilo-metres/2 miles of road were swept away, while a flood in 1989 was even more devastating, closing the lane through the valley for more than six months.

Entering the Dane Valley

Nesting curlew

The Walk

1. From the roadside car park, follow the main lane past the bridge towards the **Crag Inn**. After 50 metres turn sharp right on a track rising back across the woodland bank above the lane. At the top, fork right to **Banktop**, passing the cottage to continue across the hillside, which rises on the left to **Shutlingsloe**. The path eventually falls to meet the lane. Cross to a bridge over the river opposite and walk away at the field edge. Enter **Clough House Farm** through a gate on the left and turn right through the yard, keeping ahead beyond to a road junction.

2. Through a gate opposite, a track is signed towards the 'Cat and Fiddle Inn'. Crossing a footbridge a little way up, carry on above **Cumberland Brook** on the opposite bank, later reaching a junction by a modest waterfall.

3. Although the right branch is marked to 'Three Shire Heads', go left, still following signs to the 'Cat and Fiddle'. The path wanders on into a narrower, rocky clough, clambering beside the

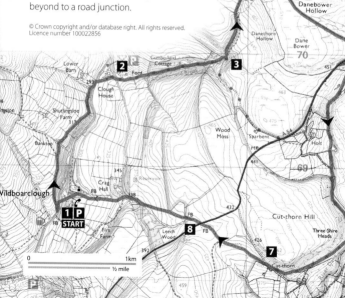

Afternoon light: *Only rushing water breaks the silence at Three Shire Heads*

stream. Higher up, cross the brook below another small cascade. The path swings left and then right to continue beside a wall. Through a gate at the top, wind across the open moor to a junction with a broad path.

4. A sign indicates that 'Three Shire Heads' lies to the right, map and sign makers disagreeing on its proper spelling. With most of the day's climbing now accomplished, you can enjoy the view across the moor to Shutlingsloe,

The Roaches and a host of lesser bumps, while ahead is the deepening fold of the upper Dane Valley.

5. Eventually reaching the road, cross and scale the crash barrier opposite. The path descends a steep bank towards the river, passing a **tall stone chimney**. (A less steep descent lies along the road to the right.) *Unrelated to the quarries on the far hillside, the chimney was part of the Dane Bower coal mine.* At the bottom of the hill, turn right through a gate, soon passing a **pit shaft entrance** and the **ruins of more pit-head buildings**.

Axe Edge glow: *I lazy evening light on the moorland path towards Danebower Hollow*

Meandering pleasantly along the valley, more or less beside the river, the path remains clear and leads to the packhorse bridge at **Three Shire Heads**, 1.6 kilometres/1 mile away.

The three shires are Cheshire, Derbyshire and Staffordshire, and this out of the way corner was often used for illicit gaming and contests. Should the police of one county arrive to put a stop to the goings on, the crowd would simply decamp across one of the borders out of jurisdiction.

6. Remaining on the western bank, continue with the track, which now turns away from the valley to climb gradually across the shoulder of the hill.

7. Meeting a lane at **Cut Thorn**, go right but leave immediately beyond the cottage over a stile on the left. Follow a trod away, rising easily across the moorland pasture. At a fork, just below a gate in a wall, bear left to meet the wall a little farther west. Crossing a stile, the path carries on across rough moss, gently descending to the **A54**.

8. Over a stile opposite, the path continues downhill, later passing through a gate and beside a small barn.

Beyond a final gate at the bottom, a short track drops at the edge of woodland to meet a lane. Turn right to a junction beside the entrance to **Crag Hall** and keep left, descending beside the stream. Lower down on the right is **St Saviour's Church** and farther on, a large house, all that remains of the valley's industry. The lane ends at the bridge opposite the car park to complete the walk. ♦

Industrial valley

During the 18th century, mechanisation brought textile production into factories, powered by swift-flowing streams such as those in the Wildboarclough valley. Crag Mill was built in 1796 and used to spin cotton and print calico and carpets. However, the introduction of steam left it uncompetitive and the buildings were demolished by 1957. Only the office block, the large house passed at the end of the walk, remains.

The dry riverbed of the River Hamps in spring

The **River Hamps**

Open hillside and wooded gorge are combined in this walk within the Hamps valley

What to expect:
A steady climb and steep descent, returning easily along the Manifold Way

Distance: 9km/ 5½ miles. Allow 2½ hours

Start: Weag's Bridge

Grid ref: SK 100 541

Ordnance Survey Map: Explorer OL24 *Peak District: White Peak area: Buxton, Bakewell, Matlock & Dove Dale*

After the walk: Tea garden at Lee House Farm OR Ye Olde Royal Oak, Wetton DE6 2AF | 01335 310287 | info@royaloakwetton.co.uk

Walk outline

Beginning from Weag's Bridge, the walk follows the Manifold Valley, but leaves opposite Beeston Tor to climb across the rolling pastures of Mere Hill. The descent to Lee House Farm by the River Hamps is steep and requires care after rain when the hillside can be slippery. The return takes the course of the short-lived Leek and Manifold Light Railway, which followed a scenic route through the Hamps valley.

River Hamps

Outside winter, you are unlikely to see much water on this walk, for the bed of the River Hamps can be largely dry; in fact its name derives from the early British word *Hanespe*, meaning 'summer dry'. The river is swallowed beneath the ground near Waterhouses and only reappears at Hamps Spring on the Manifold near Ilam. Nevertheless, the twisting gorge through which it passes is particularly pretty and was one of the delights for summer passengers on the Leek and Manifold Light Railway, which meandered through on its way to Hulme End.

Descent to the Hamps

Wild garlic or 'ramsons'

The Walk

1. From the car park, cross the lane beside **Weag's Bridge** and take the left-hand one of the two tracks opposite, which follows the course of the **River Manifold** downstream. Passing the end of a camping field, cross a bridge over the foot of the **River Hamps** and continue a little farther towards **Beeston Tor Farm**.

*The limestone caves of **Beeston Tor** have yielded many archaeological finds, including a hoard of Saxon coins and jewellery. Legend has it that the caves also gave shelter to St Bertram, an 8th-century Mercian prince. He renounced his birthright for religious piety and, like Patrick, travelled to Ireland seeking spiritual guidance. He returned with an Irish princess as his wife, but she and their baby were killed by a marauding wolf while Bertram searched for food. Distraught, Bertram turned to a life of seclusion, becoming renowned for his spiritual wisdom and ability to heal. Even in death, he was attributed with miraculous cures and his shrine at Ilam's church became a place of pilgrimage.*

2. Approaching the buildings, bear right at a fork and climb away along a stone track, signed to 'Throwley'. Keep going past a barn towards the gentle fold of the upper valley pastures. Remain with the right-hand boundary as a path is later signed away, carrying on to the corner of a wall where there is

Historic sanctuary: *Thor's Cave high in the limestone cliffs overlooking the River Manifold*

a waypost. Again stick with the wall, ascending to a gate at the top by the corner of a wood.

3. Walk on beside the trees to a second gate. Through that, turn right alongside the wall. Cresting the rise, strike away to the left across the slope of the hill, aiming for the right-hand end of a distant belt of trees. Pass the end of a broken wall and cross a stile beside a gate, ultimately reaching, by trees, a lane that comes from **Throwley Hall**.

4. Follow the lane to the right over a rise, ignoring a track from **Throwleymoor Farm**.

5. After some 550 metres and just beyond a cattle-grid, leave the lane, scaling a stile on the right. Head down the edge of the field. Over a second stile, pass through scrub beside the right boundary. The way continues steeply down into the base of the valley. Finally joining a rough track behind **Lee House Farm**, walk out over a footbridge spanning the bed of the **River Hamps**.

Opened in 1904 between Waterhouses

Into the valley: *Descending across sheep pastures into the rugged Manifold Valley*

and Hulme End, the Leek and Manifold Light Railway was intended to boost the valley's economy in which farming and copper mining were the main industries. Over summer weekends, it brought in tourists too, exchanging the drudgery of the pottery towns for a day's holiday in the country. It was a popular excursion and over bank holidays, trains sometimes ran until 10 o'clock at night. Beeston Tor and Thor's Cave were highlights of the trip and the stations there each had a refreshment room to cater for the visitors.

6. Joining the **Manifold Way**, follow it right, passing the entrance to **Lee House Farm tea garden**. The trail continues along the winding valley, repeatedly crossing the riverbed.

The limestones through which the valley courses were laid down some 340 million years ago on the bed of a warm sea, with subsequent uplift, folding and erosion creating the intricate pattern of today's valley landscape. In places such as Sparrowlee Bridge (just south of Waypoint 6), fossils from those ancient sea beds are visible in the rocks beside the trail, while caves breaking out high on the valley side were formed by underground streams

before the valley deepened to its present level. Man has been present in the valley since the end of the last ice age and Thor's Cave, ¾ mile further down the valley from the start of the walk, has revealed artefacts, human burials and animal remains as far back as the Stone Age.

Ultimately meeting the **Manifold Valley**, it then swings left back to **Weag's Bridge** to complete the walk. ♦

The Manifold Way

The Leek and Manifold Light Railway's construction along the twisting valleys was no mean feat, requiring a tunnel and seventeen river-crossings. However, despite tourism and the cheese factory at Ecton, the railway was barely profitable and survived for only 30 years. Staffordshire County Council re-opened the disused track as the Manifold Way four years later; and the eight-mile path is now one of the most popular in the area.

The famous stepping stones at Dove Dale

The **Manifold Valley**

*Two classic rivers of the Peak, the Manifold and the Dove,
brought together in a single walk*

Distance/time: 9km/ 5½ miles. Allow 3 hours

Start: Ilam Country Park, National Trust pay and display car park

Grid ref: SK 131 507

Ordnance Survey Map: Explorer OL24 *Peak District: White Peak
area: Buxton, Bakewell, Matlock & Dove Dale* AND *Explorer 259: Derby*

After the walk: National Trust visitor centre and tearoom at
Ilam Hall, Ilam E6 2AZ | 01335 350503
peakdistrict@nationaltrust.org.uk

What to expect:
*Woodland and riverside
paths; stepping-stones
(optional) or bridge*

Walk outline

*Leaving Ilam Country Park past the church and through
the village, the way climbs across rolling fields behind the
Izaak Walton Hotel into the foot of Dove Dale. After heading
upstream to cross the stepping-stones, the route returns along
the eastern bank to Coldwall Bridge past the confluence with
the Manifold. The walk then follows the southern bank of the
Dove and later the Manifold into Hinkley Wood, before finally
crossing the river and climbing back to the hall.*

The rivers Dove and Manifold

The headwaters of the rivers Dove and Manifold have
sources barely 400 metres/¼ mile apart on the edge of
Axe Moor, yet fall as two quite different valleys before
coming together below Ilam. Both rivers wind for much
of their course through deep, twisting gorges. However,
the Manifold and its main tributary, the River Hamps, both
disappear beneath ground during the summer months,
only resurfacing at Ilam. Despite it then being the larger
flow, the Manifold loses its identity to the Dove below the
confluence.

Ilam church

Meadow cranesbill

The Walk

1. A path from the corner of the car park leads towards the **National Trust tearoom and shop**. Just before reaching them, swing left beneath an archway and walk past the portico entrance to **Ilam Hall**. Leave the drive beyond the buildings on a path that takes you beside the **church**. Meeting another drive, go left and at the end, keep right, joining the lane into the village.

2. At the **memorial cross**, bear left. Abandon the lane at the edge of the village through a gate on the left onto the foot of **Bunster Hill**. Climb away right to follow a clear track across the slope of the hill. Passing through a gate, maintain the same direction across successive fields towards the flat-topped pyramidal hill of **Thorpe Cloud**. The route passes behind a farm and the **Izaak Walton Hotel**, dropping to a final stile. Beyond a fringe of trees, bear left through a car park field to emerge onto a narrow lane. To the left, it leads into **Dove Dale**, quickly degrading to a riverside track.

3. The valley bends sharply left at the foot of **Lin Dale**, where stepping-stones take the path across the river (alternatively, there is a footbridge near the car park). Follow the river back downstream on the opposite bank,

0 _____ 1km
_____ ½ mile

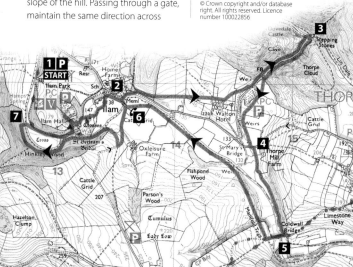

Limestone dale: *An easy path meanders up Dove Dale fringed by flower-rich 'slitherbanks'*

taking care across the foot of slither banks and on exposed rock, which may be slippery when wet. Reaching the bridge, keep ahead over a stile. Follow a trod across a meadow to a kissing-gate, rejoining the riverbank at the edge of a wooded strip. Emerging from the trees, continue across the corner of another meadow to a footbridge over a side stream and keep going, ultimately coming out onto a lane beside **St Mary's Bridge**.

4. Cross to a path diagonally opposite and head across to a gate. Bear left off the ongoing track to pick up a stream and bypass a camping field on your right. Shortly joining the **River Dove** below its confluence with the **Manifold**, walk on along a narrow meadow, eventually meeting a track beside **Coldwell Bridge**.

5. Cross the river, but just before a gate at the end of the track, go through a squeeze gap on the right. Signed to 'Ilam', a trod leads away across the undulating hillside. Pass through a

Underground river: *The 'boil hole' or resurgence of the River Manifold into the Dove*

gate into the next field, but ignore the track swinging left and carry on ahead as before. Intermittent posts mark the line of the path, which later begins to fall through scrub. Over a stile at the bottom, continue at the edge of successive fields by the **River Manifold**. In a final field, the trod shortcuts a bend of the river to a bridge at the far side, climbing out beside it onto a lane at the edge of **Ilam**.

6. Go left, soon crossing a cattle-grid and climbing onto the common. After 200 metres, opposite a footpath sign on the left, leave along a grass track on the right, which leads to a lodge gate at the edge of **Ilam Country Park**. The track runs on through **Hinkley Wood**, shortly reaching a bridge. However, remain on this bank, the ongoing path climbing through the trees above the river before dropping back to a second bridge.

7. On the far bank, cross a narrow meadow to a stile and follow a path to the right. A short way along, set back within a small enclosure is the **Battle Stone**. As the path then closes with the river, look for the **resurgence of a stream**, bubbling from the rocks

below the path and known as the 'boil hole'. The water comes from the **River Manifold**, which has gone underground upstream at Wetton Mill. Just beyond the resurgence, the path swings away from the river and zigzags up the steep bank. A gate at the top leads into the **Italian Terrace Garden**. Walk ahead, go left to the **Manifold Tearoom**, and then turn right back to the car park to complete the walk. ♦

Ilam Hall

Jesse Watts-Russell's arrival in 1820 saw massive change at Ilam. He remodelled the village in Alpine style and replaced the Tudor hall with an impressive Gothic mansion. But by the 1930s, the place had become too expensive to run, and was being demolished when it was gifted to the National Trust. What remains of the house is run as a Youth Hostel with the park open to the public.

Useful Information

Visit Peak District & Derbyshire

The Peak's official tourism website covers everything from accommodation and special events to attractions and adventure. **www.visitpeakdistrict.com**

Peak District National Park

The Peak District National Park website also has information on things to see and do, plus a host of practical details to help plan your visit. **www.peakdistrict.org**

Tourist Information Centres

The main TICs provide free information on everything from accommodation and transport to what's on and walking advice.

Bakewell	01629 816558	bakewell@peakdistrict.gov.uk
Castleton	01629 816572	castleton@peakdistrict.gov.uk
Moorland Centre	01433 670207	edale@peakdistrict.gov.uk
Upper Derwent	01433 650953	derwentinfo@peakdistrict.gov.uk

Weather

Online weather forecasts for the Peak District are available from the Met Office at **www.metoffice.gov.uk/loutdoor/mountainsafety** and the Mountain Weather Information Service at **www.mwis.org.uk/**

Rail Travel

Four railway services cross the National Park:

The Hope Valley Line

The Derwent Valley Line

The Manchester to Buxton Line

The Manchester to Glossop Line

Information is available from National Rail Enquiries on **08457 484950** or **www.nationalrail.com.uk**

Bus Travel

Peakland's towns and many of the villages are served by bus. For routes and timetables, call **Traveline** on **0871 200 22 33** or visit **www.traveline.info**